ZOOLOGY

Also by GILLIAN CLARKE
from Carcanet Press

Ice

A Recipe for Water

At the Source

Making the Beds for the Dead

Five Fields

Collected Poems

The King of Britain's Daughter

Letting in the Rumour

Selected Poems

Letter from a Far Country

GILLIAN CLARKE

ZOOLOGY

CARCANET

First published in Great Britain in 2017 by
CARCANET PRESS LTD
Alliance House, 30 Cross Street
Manchester M2 7AQ
www.carcanet.co.uk

A CIP catalogue record for this book is available
from the British Library: ISBN 9781784102166.

Book design: Luke Allan.
Printed and bound in England by SRP Ltd.

The publisher acknowledges financial assistance
from Arts Council England.

CONTENTS

I · MISSING

The Presence   13
Ghosts   14
Exhuming Your Father   15
Contre-Jour   16
Learning to Swim   17
Patagonia   18
Waves   19
Pampas Grass   20
Missing   21
The Poet   22

II · BEHIND GLASS

Silent   25
Archaeopteryx   26
Ichthyosaur   27
The Company of Bones   28
Dodo   29
Marsh Fritillaries   30
The Snowdon Rainbow Beetle   31

III · HAFOD Y LLAN

Mountain   35
Mine   36
River   37
Barracks   38
Flowers of the Mountain   39

IV · ONE YEAR

A Year at Hafod Y Llan 43

Last Gather 45

Oestrus 46

Winter 47

Alchemy 48

Old Ram 49

February 50

Scan 51

Black 52

Spring 53

Labour 54

Birth 55

Stillborn 56

Mothering 57

Dead Ewe 58

To the Mountain 59

Cynefin 60

Summer 61

The Wethers Leave the Mountain 62

September 63

V

Insect 67

Queen 68

Watchman 69

How To Put Together A Robin 70

How To Take Apart A Tree 71

The Pontfadog Oak 72

Wild Laburnum 73

Especially When the West Wind 74

Storwm Awst 76

Blind September 77

October 78

Wind 79
Damage 80
Audiology 81
Epidural 82
Cantre'r Gwaelod 83
Hafod 85
Sycharth 87
Dinefwr 88
Chawton 89
Magnetism 90
Ironing 91
Messengers 92
White Lilies 93
Where to Place a Chair 94
The Centuries' Poetry: Hopkins to Eliot 95
In A Cardiff Arcade, 1952 96
The Scribe 97
Words 98

VI · ELEGIES

The Blackbird 101
The Brown Hare 103
Barley 104
Eisteddfod of the Black Chair 105
Last Letter Home 106
Madiba 107
Daughter 108
Olwen 109
Birdsong 110
Flight 111
New Moon 112

Notes 115
Acknowledgements 117

ZOOLOGY

I

MISSING

A small wind winds through rush and sedge,
movement, heartbeat halts at the edge
of the lawn, stillness of hinged limbs
under the oak's November flame.

Something powers the morning, stops the air,
holds me in the planet of its stare,
its silence, not gunshot and the scream
I heard once, waking from a dark dream

in another place, but a pulsing presence
red-brown beneath the trees, a sense
that such a living thing once seen
in that sunlit space will never be gone,

its breath a mist on the air
between field and lawn. There. Not there.

A cindering sound of rain comes in from the sea
over someone's fields and someone else's farms,
over the roads and little lanes leading to us,
fleeced, waterproof sheep sipping the grass,
the sandstone terrace dancing with broken sky,
the ocean hush and shift of foliage;

and everyone ever here is here again, now:
my mother, her luminous beauty marred
by hands that plunged in too much earth,
nail-bitten, rough with mending and peeling,
hot-water-scrubbing, loving a garden and house,
fingering leaves of the acer we planted for her;

your father, his miner's hands gnarled as the oak
we planted in his name; its leaves are falling gold
through the gap in the hedge-bank where something
spindles the long lean of its limbs, there,
stilled between acer and oak and it is always
now, and all of them always here, alive:

my Ga whose hands spun lace from Pembrokeshire tides;
my aunt who gave me poetry, word and world;
my father who conjured Welsh, a fox cub, a rabbit
from his sleeve, and lifted me onto the sill that night
in the war, sky roaring with planes over the sea
to France, saying 'Never forget this sight.'

They walk towards me over the fields,
through the gate and the gap in the hedge
where the hare comes halting when I look up,
where I'll walk home to you.

Somewhere in a graveyard in broken Greece,
a man leans on his grief. A shovel, gloves,
a plastic bag. He doesn't own this plot
and the three-year rent is up. One he loves
lies here, in a few cubic metres of earth.
He brings the dead one, like another birth,

lifts the beloved, once father, once man,
reduced to a gather of earth and bone,
skull empty of all memory and mind,
the scattered fingers of a father's hand,
the all-is-forgiven warmth of their last hold
hardly faded from a son's reminding,

the loosening, letting go. His hands curl
on pins and needles, pearls.

From where he stands inside the cave,
my invisible father, the camera's eye
sees a radiant gash in rock, a doorway
open to sea and sky,

a boat beached on pebbled silver,
the tide a brilliance ebbing at the brink
of blackness. And who is she who leans
on the tilt of the stern?

So often we rowed over the bay, slow
slap of the swell, lift and dip of the prow,
to drift close to the dark door, and call
through the portal into the underworld,

to hear our voices, smaller, smaller, as if
swallowed by the silence of the cliff.

He taught me to swim, his palm a saucer.
When I wasn't looking he let me go
to the slippery hands of the sea,
to level myself by the dipping, rising horizon,
to gravity, buoyancy, and the ocean gods.

*

I swim far out across the bay.
Black cliffs rise sheer out of green water
where light is blond over drowned sand,
crevices secret in their mermaid hair.
Sand-martins touch and go, electric,
as if sunlight made rock burn.

I'm cold as sand. In the cave's throat
a breath of samphire, the sunken wreck
in which I'm trapped in dreams
where, in a fishtail gleam
she leans to kiss me as she goes
dressed in her beauty to a Christmas dance.

The tide lifts and lets go. Nothing
breaks the surface of darkness or sea
where we beached the boat so long ago,
and I suddenly knew she slipped him,
that he carried like an x-ray
her shadow picture.

The year he didn't die,
he left on a banana boat
to convalesce at sea,
left me in teenage rage.

From his ocean-lit cabin, rocked
by the sleepless motion of waters,
he sent us deeps and shallows, shoals
and shinings in blue envelopes, the fin

of a whale breaking the surface where the nib
turned, his lines of longhand rolling
across fine pages, regular
as the sea's unfolding story.

Where are they now, those letters
like poetry of the sea?
I think she burnt them, feeding her need
to be free of it all.

Left, his voice on tape, found in his office
after the funeral, those interviews
from Patagonia in a strange Welsh,
his voice not like himself.

After sixty years I hear it better
in my head: '*Hwyl fawr*,' he says to me,
last words, clear as a ship's bell,
before he turns to leave.

WAVES

When long ago my father cast his spell
with wires and microphones, he told me
he could send sound on waves the speed of light
to touch the ionosphere and fall
home to the wireless on our windowsill.

Sometimes, radio on, half listening, struck still
by a line of verse, a voice, a chord, a cadence,
I think of living light in a breaking wave,
not breath, not fire, not water, but alive,
the sudden silver of a turning shoal,

and I still see words on the radio as birds
or fish homing to settle in the hush
of long waves on a beach in Pembrokeshire,
a staircase in the sea, or in the air,
space humming with murmurations of words.

I'm five, and looking after my father.
I hold his hand. The house has a white gate.
There's a signpost with a name I can't say.
He says, 'We're going to see a friend.'
Inside his voice a secret silence,
like the water table he explained to me.

At the door's a tall man, his pretty wife.
The baby smells of milk. I'm sent to play.
My father's voice is making something better.
The man's in the RAF. I saw him
talking to my mother and her friend,
the one whose sweetheart died in the war.

There is no undercurrent I can't hear,
no murmur I miss in the hum and purr
of grown-up silences, not words out loud
but river-rumour running underground,
or voices behind glass when no-one speaks
the words their faces tell.

By the gate's a plant I name for the place
whose word on the signpost I can't say.
I stroke the plumes, silk-sound in my hands,
singing like tails of mountain ponies,
or water-talk you almost understand,
Aberga-feathers shedding words on the wind.

I remember Sundays,
the effort to be ordinary,
the wedding cutlery
freed from its velvet and satin.
He in his basement workshop,
sanding, sawing, singing,

she, hot in the kitchen
queen of the hour, the day,
two-way Family Favourites
to the percussion of pans,
steam and sweet aromas,
her altar of damask and silver,

he an absence, underground,
or his name called down the garden
when the mower stops.
While she carves the roast
I hear his steps on gravel
or the basement stairs,

his hands under running water,
not arrived, sitting down,
just his empty chair,
and she saying,
'Don't wait for your father.
Don't let it get cold.'

THE POET

*Beth yw gweithio ond gwnaed cân
o'r coed a'r gwenith?*

(*What is work but making a song
from the wood and the wheat?*)

WALDO WILLIAMS

We pause on the bend of the stony track
to look at the sea. He lifts me
onto the gate, in his pocket an apple
for the milk-horse. Its breath is a field.
A fist of hay, the pushy, plushy muzzle
fizzes my palm with spit.

Over horizons of gate, field, sea,
I watch for stories, for the giant Brân
to wade though the sea towing his fleet,
for the starling to whisper my name,
for the old milk-horse to carry us
galloping over the fields.

I dream we're flying – when my father
turns, greeting a man on the track, not Brân,
just 'Mr Williams, the poet', a man
whose name I'd forgotten, but now remember:
that day, words between then and forever,
songs of the wood and the wheat.

II

BEHIND GLASS

these creatures,
leatherback turtle, dolphin, killer whale,
python, iguana, komodo dragon,

the generations in their glass houses,
insect, mammal, reptile, bird,
with nothing to say for themselves.

In the stone, a bird skeleton spread
in a scrabble of earth before flight,
stopped in a moment of mud-flow, lava, flood.

The dead here live forever
in their stillness.
They have gone as far as they can.

Will we be this beautiful when we pass
into the silence, behind glass?

The first bird in the world
stilled in stony silence in its case.
Flight feathers, wishbone, that perching foot,
lost in the limestone of a salt lagoon, a mould
from the Jurassic, print, exactitude,
a frozen moment in Earth's book of stone,
transition between dinosaur and bird,
memory of wing-feathers, skull and bones,
impression left by a magpie on the lawn,
bump-landing, lift-off, touch and go,
its wing-beats leaving angels in the snow
an icy hour before dawn.
                    First bird,
thence every warbler, song thrush, wren,
the blackbird in the ash, five notes repeating
                    again, again, again.

ICHTHYOSAUR

Jurassic travellers
trailing a wake of ammonites,
the loosed flotilla of her vertebrae
stilled in the current.

Behind glass she dies giving birth.
Millions of years too late
it can still move us,
the dolphin-flip of her spine

and the frozen baby turning its head
to the world at the last moment
as all babies do, choked
as it learned to live.

like a lamb at the field-edge
born the wrong way up
or strangled at birth
by the mothering cord.

As he ducked under her lintel,
earth slapped on them a burning hand,
leaving a grace of bones
eloquent in stone.

Orangutan, Chimpanzee, Gorilla, Man
have kept me company for days here in the silence,
glass and the ages, wastes of ice between us.

On the table, touchable, molar of mammoth, mandible
of wolf, humerus of bear, skull of reindeer,
one antler still attached,

and elk, short antler-beams
before palmation, high nasal bones, long snout
to forage in its arboreal home.

Yet again and again I return to this little dancer,
the golden lion tamarin, *leontopithecus rosalia,*
small as a cat stilled in its beautiful bones,

twenty-six joints in the engineered curve of its tail,
then the spine to anchor pelvis, neck, skull,
the breathless cage of its ribs, the heart's stopped clock,

my own heart working the blood through my wrist,
my breath in my hand, like the tamarin's hand,
and the hand of Orangutan, Chimpanzee, Gorilla, Man.

DODO

What is left of this bird but a word for loss
and a thousand bones in the mire of Mare aux Songes?
'Wallowbird', 'fulsome foule twice as big as a swan',

prodigious pigeon, she flew across warm seas
under the Southern Cross in the world's emptiness
lonely ages ago, fed on fruits of paradise,

forgot how to fly, laid her single egg on a nest
of sticks, warmed it to hatch under her breast.
Imagine first meeting of hen and chick, and last.

Her cry's lost on the wind; feathers, flesh
rot in the swamp of dreams. What might have been
just bones found in the mud by human feet –

skull, scapula, vertebrae, toes – each a hieroglyph
of the alphabet by which we read the myth.

MARSH FRITILLARIES

Eurodryas aurinia

A drawer of frozen butterflies,
each impaled on the tiny stilt of its pin,
as numerous as those quivering, alive
in the colonies on Cors Llawr Cwrt, larvae
that live on devil's bit scabious on the bog.
They hunger, eat, belong, mate, breed and die.
I love their language, pupae, chrysalides,
the coloured oculi that dot their wings,
their almost symmetry, their beauty
nourished on buttercup, betony, bugle,
sprung from the hoofprints of grazing cattle
on wetland and marsh. Though none here stir
under the glass, they could be alive.
If I gaze long enough, they move.

THE SNOWDON RAINBOW BEETLE

Chrysolina cerealis

Trapped like the Snowdon lily when ice lost its grip
as loosening glaciers began to slip,
mountains to give way with a slow, deep groan,
scouring valleys from the tuffs and ash
of old upheavals, this creature went its own way.
It survives on Snowdon's western flanks,
feeding on flowers of the wild thyme.
Genetically distinct, a jewel.
its elytra striped with copper, gold,
precious metals of the mountain, emerald,
blue of the inky *llyn*, the colour of slate
in rain.
   What's beauty for, but to disguise
a beetle as a waterdrop to hold
Snowdonia in a carapace of gold?

III

HAFOD Y LLAN

This place has secrets,
tunnels into the black seep and drip,
under roots of trees, into the stone womb
past wheels, pulleys, chains, trucks locked
in their pollens of rust.

Deep as the Ordovician, old workings,
mineshafts, mullock heaps, piles of slag,
abandoned two centuries back, river-stones
stained blue with copper, copper-iron's gold,
sulphates from the mountain's heart.

MINE

By torchlight a stream
hangs three hundred feet
in glassy stillness.
Ferns sip sunlight at a rock fissure,

where the miner waded
to the knees in ice,
where darkness laps at the brink
of a void deep as cathedrals,

where rungs crook rusted fingers over the drop,
his heart and candle guttering,
where his foot felt for a hold in air,
his hand on rock slimed by centuries of rain,

where the falling stone of his cry
is echoing still.

The current does a double-turn
under the bridge, about the boulder,
black water in a sleeve of silver,
light's italics at the rock's shoulder.

Ages of ice and water made this place,
seepage of springs, a gleam of streams
rising from mist and murk as flood
meets deep and secret aquifers.

Blue with copper, Craflwyn's waters
smoothed boulders for gateposts, walls,
a corner-stone for a farm, slipped blades of ice
between the slate so it splits clean as a page.

Weather, miner, shepherd, farmer made this place,
worked the slopes, hollowed the heart of it,
plundered its power, built *hafod* and *hendre,*
turned water into fire, roofed Europe with slate.

BARRACKS

The moan of wind in these stones
is the lonely monotone
of men, half dreaming, half awake
under the weight of longing
for a wife in their aching arms;

for pain to lift from their bones;
to exchange the shouldered burden of slate,
the cold, the wet, six days a week,
for the gift of belonging
a few Sunday hours in her arms.

In Arctic scree, sandstone, granite, quartzite:
parsley fern, fir clubmoss, woolly fringe moss,
liverwort, wavy hair grass, fescue, foxglove,
heath bedstraw, heather, bilberry, myrtle,

crevice communities of ferns, mosses,
lichens, Arctic saxifrage, maidenhair,
spleenwort, liverwort, the brittle blade fern,
and high in rocky Alpine clefts too steep

for sheep, under the shadow of peregrine,
chough, ring ouzel, hen harrier, merlin,
unique on earth, the Snowdon lily
trembles in genuflection to the wind.

IV

ONE YEAR

The weather turns. The wind's Atlantic,
wild, without winter's bite.
Sheep stand, backs to the wind,
gather in the lee of fallen walls,
each scrawl of stone a demarcation,
an edge of something, someone's land.

Walls centuries-old, wind-ruined, rain-loosened,
fixed, frost-fingered to rubble,
made good again, again
by generations of hard hands.
Thorn trees lean wind-stripped,
stooped ghosts of the old wall-menders.

saf yna! tyrd yma! cer ti ôl!
gan bwyll, gan bwyll! i'r de, i'r de.

At the call dogs streak to the slope.
A single ewe on the track, another,
a gather, a rosary of sheep, strands
threading their way from ridge and crag
from *bwlch* and *cwm*, *crib* and *carreg*

silent and far, the hefted flock
sleeving silver like mountain streams,
chorus and choir of ewe and lamb:
Song of the mountains, a drumming
in the air, on the track.

cân o'r mynyddoedd, sŵn drwmio,
yn yr awyr, ar y trac

Dogs and sheep in the dance of the slopes,
the mountain deep in animal brain,
hefting the weight, treading the shape of it,
cynefin in their bones, nerves, blood.

Listen! to the gathering beat
of their feet on the path.
The mountain strums with streams,
falls mass force, its cavernous heart
pounding with underground rivers,
with the sound of hoof-beats on the track,
of water deep in the rock
of wind in the slate mines.

sŵn traed defaid ar y llwybrau,
sŵn dŵr dwfn dan y mynydd,
sŵn y gwynt ym mhyllau'r llechi,

The mountain is humming:
cân bûr o bŵer yn Afon Cwmllan,
yn alcemi o ddŵr a thrydan
pure song of power in the river Cwmllan,
alchemy of water turned to fire.

October, and the mountain is a river,
the flock fluent on the slopes,
a commotion of cries,

the mountain lament's
a high chorus of lambs,
the ewes' deep descant.

After summer on the mountain
they gather to be penned,
separated, driven apart,
lamb from ewe.
They will cry all night,
lamb-grief and mother-grief.

In November's narrowing light
before the darkest day, before first fall
of winter snow, the rams are turned out dancing
to run the slopes with the ewes.

In shortening days, reducing light,
her chemistry stirs, sleeping hormones wake
in her brain's dark chamber, and she's ready,
restless again for the scent of the ram.

On heat she greets him, sniffs him to be chosen.
The ewe takes the ram, and something quickens
in the secret dark, a sensed flowering,
a difference in the pulse of things,

multiplying and dividing cells,
ova, zygote, embryo, foetus, lamb,
an unstoppable force strong
as the river in the mountain's heart.

To him it is lightning,
brainstorm, hunger.
To her it is all things.
It is the future.

Thunder in the mountain,
thunder in the stones,
old thunder in the mineshafts,
in the bloodstream, in the bones,

in the caves where rivers start,
in the womb where life begins
like a match struck in the dark.

Breath of the white dragon,
a first flake of snow.
Another, another, feathers
dissolve on the tongue of a ewe,
cwtched in the lee of a crag.

Then more, faster, swarming, till world is blind,
silent, walled in, wall-eyed, the flock a drift
against stone, fleece under fleece of snow.
The ice-moon's breath turns all to glass.
Where is warm? Where is grass? Where is light?

All the short hours of day, hunger-driven,
hoofing the frozen ground
she grazes for a scrape of green,
the one place bare of snow
where she has lain.

Inside the snow, the fleece. Inside the fleece,
something beating in its house of bone.
Cold draws on every organ but the womb.
Rocked in its cradle in the blood-loud dark.
the foetus, safe in its rose-red room.

All night the moon stares at the stream
strumming its way over stones,
stopping it dead in its dream;
gazes at the field's ghost
where all the white night long
no mouse, fox, hare has passed.

Moon, witch, goddess, alchemist, old stone,
strikes trees to iron, silver, steel, stills sheep
where they stand asleep in their bones,
till dawn, the sun on the sill of the world,
when all the night-work of the moon
is hallowed, haloed, turned to gold.

There is death on the mountain,
where a ram undressed his bones,
a weft of stems in the warp of his ribs,
ligaments undone by rain.

Gutted by foxes, crows,
disrobed by birds for spring nests,
he has spilled himself; his fluids
flood the mountain stream.

His eye is the *Snowdon lily*,
death gapes in his quarried face,
spiders spin his skull's shroud,
crows cry down the *cwm* of his horns.

In spring he came over Crib Goch,
a young moon rising,
the flower of his seed
whitening Eryri.

Like an old farm gone to earth,
slipped stone by stone, lost
to the power of time to undo a wall,
of *hafod* and *hendre*, *'scubor* and *beudy*.

Ravens sign the sky. Buzzard and crow
circle, thirsting for a lamb's eye.
A vixen too has her children,
waiting hungry in the earth.

Y mis bach, the little month,
between the end and the beginning,
between the dark and the light.

Each day the mountain
draws back its shadow from the valley
minutes sooner.

In day's widening arc
more seconds for a pregnant ewe
to stand at her grazing.

Before the running dogs, the whistles and the calls,
the ewe follows the flock down for scanning.

She walks into the trap,
a scanner to the vulva, to the womb.
The machine spies with its little eye.
Her story is a barcode.

The scanner eyes the womb.
Cells have multiplied,
the buds of limbs,
the casket of a skull.

The shadow of a single foetus –
a good ewe sent unmarked
to winter in sheltering valley fields,
at Hafod, Faenol, Tremadog.

The lamb unfolding in her womb
will birth in valley pastures
where the river runs black
between fields of melting snow.

BLACK

Branded black, the 'empty' ewes,
corralled in Cae Dan Wal,
the field under the wall,
bearing their nothing like a stone.

The womb clenches like a heart
against the void, as they wait,
weighted, for a journey,
hollow on the holy hill.

They are barren, empty,
without foetus, without future,
the end of the line,
the last cord cut.

SPRING

After frozen ground, a loosening.
After silence, birdsong, a beginning.
Earth's skin pricks with growth.

Snows melt and flow,
filling streams, falls, rivers,
streaking the slopes.

A wing of light spreads, rises
up, up the mountain slopes.
Fields flood with green.

LABOUR

One ewe alone in the field corner
turning, turning, hoofing the ground.
Leave her to it. She knows best the meaning
of the womb's upheavals,

knows it like the mountain,
like the sounding waters in the earth
drumming the rock beneath her feet,
the pounding of her own heart,

and the heart of the other,
beating beneath hers,
the one she'll birth tonight
to her body's own wild music.

BIRTH

Black early hours, a first tidal surge
rocks the lamb in its red cave.
The ewe turns, turns, hoofing the earth,
then down again, head up, stargazing.
A long low groan and she's on her feet,
pausing to pull grass.

This is new – the lamb uncurls
in the pulsing dark, chin on its knees,
fore-hooves step for a journey.
A ripple, a riptide, a breaking
of waters, and a great muscular heave
whelms them both, ebbs and rises

again, again, a tide lifting them in a storm
of pain, of need, impulse and instinct,
till the lamb is birthed like a fish
steaming in moonlight,
and gives one broken cry
at being alive.

STILLBORN

Another ewe calls by the hedge.
Something is too still on the earth.
Is this birth, or death?

She licks the corpse to life,
love's chemistry raging
in her blood, her brain?

She licks, licks, obsessed.
She drinks it, smells it.
It is hers, this death in birth.

She thirsts for her lamb, stillborn, still warm,
licks him clean with a growl of love.

He shepherds her into the shed,
turns her head away,

steals the corpse and rips,
the hiss of the blade a single tear, throat to tail.

The stripped flesh is steam in icy air,
a delta of veins and marbled rose,

the months inside her growing to this:
flesh veined like a petal, a butterfly's wing,

still salt from the sea of her womb,
a perfect thing, done-for, food for the vixen.

Quick as a thief take his torn-off coat
and swaddle a stolen twin in this shawl of blood.

Hold her head. Let it suckle her.
Let them both know hunger,

he for the milk, she fooled by the smell and taste
of what she has borne and birthed in the dark.

In the lee of a broken wall,
an old ewe weakened by winter
and the needy foetus under her heart.

They'll throw what's left of her into the truck
like the millions cast on the pyre
in the days of the virus.

What wounds is the tender glimpse,
like a sanctuary lamp,
of the vulva's unfolding rose,

and thought of the secret lamb,
cold, heart-stopped
in the funeral boat of her body.

TO THE MOUNTAIN

Along the road to the mountain track,
a commotion of ewe song, psalm of the flock,
a panic of lambs losing, finding
by smell and by sound like mother and child
holding hands in a crowd.

It quietens as the flock finds its way,
the track under-hoof, the old mountain
learned and remembered now and forever,
in the line, in the blood, in the grain
of the breed, passed ewe to lamb.

Summer's slow and easy,
long mothering days on the mountain,
to teach, to learn the *cynefin*:
laid down in the brain, blood, belonging,
belief, tribal memory, and land,
heft, habit, *hiraeth*, heart and hearth,
passed through generations;

more than a map – a sense of place,
or a moment's sudden gold
on a mountain peak,
when sheep or shepherd, human or beast
know this for certain: here, now, I belong.
It is my place: *cynefin*.

SUMMER

Long hours of daylight
flood the horizons of her pupils,
fill her brain with sleepy golden light,
quell the chemistry of desire
till her season comes again.

New wool, like a veil of snow,
spreads over naked skin,
over scrapes and ridges where the blade cut close.
It will thicken and grow dense, a quilt
for her body and the lamb it will bear.

Late summer and young wethers gathering,
lament of lamb-bleat and ewe-cry
that held them together since spring
is a broken choir. Evening echoes with grief,
ewes hopelessly calling their lambs.

By dawn the mountain is calm again,
sheep grazing long shadows in the rising sun.

The cycle begins again.
The weather turns. The wind's Atlantic.

Cân o'r mynyddoedd,
sŵn drwmio, yn yr awyr, ar y trac.

Song of the mountains, drumbeat
in the air, on the track.

V

INSECT

Over the black granite worktop
where I polish the fossilised dead,
a creature too small to discern
dances on shimmering wings.

Don't set down a plate, a pot
till it's safely flown.
Don't let the light of the world be less
by a single glimmering thing.

QUEEN

Ice has locked the frozen garden
these cold days of December.
The stone man's shawled and cowled.
The iron man's lap's a brim of cold.
Inside, lamps lit for evening, the room warms,
flames climb in the stove, and nightly

she walks, stirred from the hushed dust
of a curtain-fold, steps out to preen,
summer's future in her winter dream.
We're careful not to crush or brush aside
the pregnant queen. She clings to my finger
as I set her safe beside my open book,

settles herself in yellow lamplight
to clean her six hinged limbs,
abdomen, mandibles, helmet of black and gold,
multiple eyes, thorax, wings of spun glass
veined like petals of wild plum, quince,
apple trees fertilised on humming days.

Her wintering body's a citadel
of a thousand cells. In spring she'll build
her palace from spittle and cellulose
scraped from the timbers of our house,
and lay her eggs in a thousand cradles
pulsing with the humdrum psalm of summer.

WATCHMAN

The Newport Ship, sixteenth-century, discovered 2002

In perpetual dusk, in the shallows
of a tank in an industrial shed, a shadow,

a loneliness I can't quite sense
or put a name to; a dark silence

slow as cloud. The shadow stirs
in murky water, creature, stranger,

nightwatchman, grazer of estuaries, scourer
of an old ships' bones in this watery harbour,

it feeds on micro-organisms brought ashore
from burial in the mudbanks of the Usk.

A great ship lifted, board by strut by spar
out of six hundred years of river mud,

a ghost of wind in its sails and a hushing ocean,
subdued in a tank, in the watch of a sturgeon.

It takes four hands to mend a robin
snagged in this snare, a tangle of netting
draped to keep birds off the blueberries.

You cradle the bird, its heart wild in your hand,
its breath a puff in your palm, your soul
a flame in the planet of its eye.

I learn a bird's anatomy as I go,
finger the rosary of vertebrae.
wishbone, the sternum's keel – bird bones

are tubes of air – find where to cut, where free,
snip, unknot, follow a snarl of thread
biting each wing, the bible-paper skin.

It lies frozen, fearing, trusting us,
paramedics in a race with death
bearing a broken child. It takes an hour,

my life in its eye till the last thread's cut,
and you step out under the sky,
open your hands, and let it fly.

The old chestnut is dead. Mossed, bark-stripped,
it must be felled, wind-filled sails brought down,
the tree dismantled, its shadow scoured
from the house-wall, with the mould-grey ghost
sun couldn't reach nor rain rinse clean.

Untie the washing line where pegged-out sheets
pulled to sea when the wind turned westerly.
Let the rising sun pour gold through un-blind
morning windows. Give the east wind
no instrument to strum on winter nights.

Begin with a branch. The surgeon leans back
from the trunk in his sling and takes it
piece by piece apart with his whining saw
letting each limb fall, the dismembered dead.
Pity the fallen. Trailer them away.

He leaves the limbless trunk to the axe,
gnomon and shadow, standing stone.
Its populations leave their fallen city,
woodlice, woodwasps, beetles, ants
bearing their living and their dead.

Respect the old tree's bones, stow log and branch
for winter fires, email the children:
'Your tree is gone.' Spring rains will rinse the wound.
Sunlight will dress the scar in rising grasses,
foxtail and fescue, quaking grass and bent.

THE PONTFADOG OAK

c. 802–2013

Quercus, *derwen*, sacred druid tree,
rings of history scribed in its heartwood,
stood its ground twelve centuries,
anchored by old roots and its own weight.

Twelve hundred years of leafing and unleaving,
of blackbirds' nests, pied flycatchers, a living
insect citadel, each crack and crevice
a *cwtch* for wintering wrens and honey bees,

its hollow heart a cave for lovers,
cell for the holy, shelter for sheep, cover
for soldier, thief, fugitive, conspirator,
a place of tryst, trust, betrayal. Older

than cathedrals, its branches caught the stars,
made cruck and cradle, roof beams, rafters,
fuel for the hearth; pollarded, sprouted, spared
when Henry Plantagenet rased Ceiriog woods.

In 1165, the midnight bell-note of the owl
from its branchy tower the rallying call
when Owain Gwynedd roused his men
for victory at Crogan against the Saeson.

Ten centuries on, an April wind
brought down the king of trees. It fell unseen,
laying its branches, just beginning to green,
on Cilcochwyn's slates, slack as a dead hand.

As May tilts into June the land's on fire,
farms folded deeper into rings
of wild laburnum, *tresi aur*,
fields encircled with gold, and summer air

yellow with yeasty leavening.
Step out. Inhale its musk
in evening's lengthening light
when other colours have dissolved in dusk.

Dark will follow this delicious hour.
In a week sills, roof, drive, gutters
will be inlaid gold with fallen flowers,
tresses turning to sour rosaries,

poisonous pods ignored by grazing herds.
Relish, before the blackbird's nest is cold,
and he sings no more in the ash,
and we've spent the gold.

ESPECIALLY WHEN THE WEST WIND

after Dylan Thomas

Especially when the west wind rises
far out in the Atlantic breathing salt
to write in longhand on the pond,
scrawl skies with paragraphs of birds,
herd huddled sheep against the hedge,
spell sibilance in rushes, reeds and sedge,
under dark murmurations of words
scoring each page of darkening skies;

when the heart quickens at crows shaken
out of the air, a flam-buoyance of kites,
gulls thrown to sea like flights of angels;
when the careful garden's taken apart,
death-decomposing and returned to earth;
when the devil's in the blackberries
left ungathered; when words drift in flurries,
trees undone to die before rebirth.

Imagine: Gone. Stopped heart, mind silent,
wordless songs a wind won't wake
or wild Atlantic weather break
over this hill, this roof, this house,
no dying light, or loose-gold-falling
leaves, no weather, day or night,
no season shortening or narrowing light,
no coming winter, following spring.

After the shortest day, the longest night.
With the first fall of January snow
come all remembered winters long ago,
dark world's transfiguration white

as the first page. Alive in the dying year, I make
my music out of words the wind shakes
from the wild sky whatever the season,
whatever weather over the heart breaks.

When the blackbird listens on the lawn, head cocked
in August silence, for the smallest syllable
of the worm; when heat gathers, darkening;
when skies growl and the *storwm Awst*
begins iambic drumming on the slates,
whispering water-vowels in the trees;

when tractor wheels rhyme tracks across the land
and the homeless hare's a gold initial
on the lawn's page, and red kites fork
their fire in the air above mown fields;
when big machines have combed cut grasses
bloody with crushed creatures into rows;

when the weather is Atlantic, the season mellowing,
and trees wait weighted with assonance of rain,
when storm-blown flocks of birds are paragraphs
and the wind writes in italics over water,
and the heart's beat is a spell spelling itself,
then might words catch fire, and world rhyme.

BLIND SEPTEMBER

After a summer of rain –
downpours drumming road and roof,
a skelter of squalls out of the blue,
gurgling in gutter and drain –

open doors and windows
to a still September.
Only the robin sings now –
birds and children have flown,

and this is how yellow feels
your two hands filled with gold,
sun on your face,
first leaves underfoot.

And this is the touch of blue, breath
of an autumn garden,
wetness of dewy webs,
from the slippery silk of hydrangea.

Taste it dark in the purple fall of a plum
in the smell of new cut grass,
the lawnmowers' evensong,
and blackberry beads bursting on the tongue.

The trees are closing down
in leaf-dropping silence,
cutting the sap from each stem,
closing capillaries, the throats of roots.
The lawn spreads open its palm
for the collection, a pyx of coins.

Eight decades of Octobers –
not that I noticed most years –
not always as slow, slant, silent
a season, as going, going, gone,
so lovely I could be seven, eight,
counting the gold, the conkers,

missing not one, not a small one,
not a fat polished warm-in-the-palm one
still in its helmet, the mother-cup,
milky, lint-wombed and clean,
and the silk sound of brush on stone
as I sweep the leaves.

WIND

Thirty years in this house and never before
such a howl of rage in the trees, a plundering palaver,
world upside-down, stampeding herds of cloud
blowing biblical nostrils of wind in a thunder

of hoof and harrumph. One shouldering shove,
pots grappled to ground, trees heave their roots,
pond water wakes, scared to a running tide,
rose-arch felled with its bells of birdseed, nuts.

Something's unhinged in a tantrum of drums,
as ridge-tiles take to the sky, fly, fall,
stone on stone, clattering scatter of bits,
in one long howling brute Atlantic hum.

and a hundred metres down through the gap
in the hedge, like a rip of lightning,
the tunnel gives way with a growl,
one wild white shoulder raised –

the blazing wing of an angel of wrath –
and you, like Jacob, must wrestle it down
with ropes, breezeblocks, bricks, beams and bars,
nailing God to the earth.

DAMAGE

Rough-midwifed out of the womb,
ripped through the bloody wound,
syllable-spine and sapling lily-bones
hauled from a lap of blood-waters, warm

into an outrage of sound, skin, nerve,
electric out of the dark, whole – save
the hidden tear in my newborn limb,
found after walking the earth all my life.

On the screen, a scar, crow on a wire,
scored word on the cochlea of a baby
born to war, or a gun fired too close
that summer of skies crying out loud

when bombers roared the cradled corridors
spiralling down the ear's conch, scorching
newborn skin, till a lifetime later the scar
surfaces, a blemish, blurring sound.

He gives me a pair of tiny microphones
to step out and try. The world's too loud.
Trees talk to the wind; tyres complain
in the rain. Water is speaking in tongues.

They all talk at once, the living, the dead.
commotions of clouds, crowds, words,
rumour of poets long gone, the rhyme,
and, when I lie in bed in the dark, the hum,

the echoing sound
of the universe born before time,
still shaking the ground.

A boat afloat on a river,
vertebrae loosed, lost,
a broken rosary scattered
at the edge of the current,

stilled, adrift, stalled in a dream –
a world seen through water, arms loose as oars,
the rowlocks of shoulder blades holding them slack;
hands are paddles stroking the stream,

knee, fragments picked from the flood,
knobs of femur, tibia, the patella
a porcelain piece found on the shore
and kept just in case,

and through and beyond the waterfall,
green-chasubled priests,
bowing, blurred, prayerful,
attend to their ministries,

like the day at Hirwaun we stood stunned
under the fall of the river,
pockets full of flowers, feathers, bird bones,
the skull of a hare, the scream still inside it.

The morning after, the beach at Borth
is a graveyard, a petrified forest
thundered out of the sand by the storm,
drowned by the sea six thousand years ago
when the Earth was flat,
the horizon the edge of the world.

Remains of stilted walkways tell their story:
how she walked over water between trees,
longing for land lost when the sea-god stole it,
fled with her children, shouldered, shawled,
with every creature that could crawl, run, fly,
till time turned truth to myth.

It's how it will be as world turns reflective:
seas sated with meltwater, craving more;
a cliff-fall takes a bungalow; a rising
tide rips up a coastal train-track;
storm fells a thousand-year-old oak,
smashes a graceful seaside promenade.

Grieve for lost wilderness – for the lovesick salmon
lured by sweet river-water sleeved in the salt,
homing upstream to spawn at the source
where it was born; for mating hares
in love with the March wind; for thermals
lifting a flaunt of red kites over the wood;

for bees mooning for honey in weedless fields;
for sleepy Marsh Fritillary butterflies
swarming the ancient bog of Cors Llawr Cwrt;
for the Brown Hairstreak in love with blackthorn

and the honeydew of aphids in the ash;
for the blackbird's evening aria of possession;

for Earth's intricate engineering, unpicked
like the bones, flesh, sinews of the mother duck
crushed on the motorway, her young
bewildered in a blizzard of feathers;
the balance of things undone by money,
the indifferent hunger of the sea.

HAFOD

'Old houses were scaffolding once and workmen whistling.'

T. E. HULME

Stand here, where Coleridge might have stood,
summer, seventeen ninety-four, high
on a mountain road where the wind steps
under a lonely arch beneath an apse
of cloud. No estate now, no wall, no gate,
just an empty road threading its stone eye.

I came here, to Cwm Ystwyth, long ago,
Hafod a ruin then, a wind-filled hulk
of the glory it was, burnt, rebuilt, fallen
to the rat, the barn owl and the crow,
gone to winter rain and frost, a skull
for plunder and the demolition ball.

We dream what we hear and see, but wilder,
a house long lost in trees, ghostly and colder
where a poem might be born. Coleridge
that summer, on his mountain walking tour,
pausing on the road to Devil's Bridge,
and I see what he, surely, saw:

Thomas Johnes' great house beside the river,
Hafod, its towers and walls, its pleasure-dome,
octagonal library of rare volumes,
raised here in the valley of the Ystwyth,
among young groves of oak and beech,
slopes of Scots pine and sapling larch.

Coleridge conjured paradise on laudanum –
but memory's a snowstorm in a globe, and mind

a cavern measureless to man where the wind
might wail for a demon lover, almost human,
and Ystwyth's 'sun-glittering waters' are a stream
conjured by poetry, not an opium dream.

SYCHARTH

House of hearth and heart, of generous board,
great halls flame-lit for feasting, harp and bard
under crucks and crossbeams cut from forest oak,
and from its chimneys, slow cats'-tails of smoke.

Nine halls of harmony for string and voice,
penillion of poets, a brimming chalice.
All gone. All gone to ground, and Owain's *Plas,*
his fine *llys* on the hill lies under grass.

The roots of trees reach deep
and Sycharth's scarred earth sleeps
under sheep-nibbled hilly quilts of lawn.
A dream stillborn, and Owain gone

to some anonymous grave, a princedom broken,
and a country taken.

DINEFWR

The valley is a page under the sky's
scriptorium, where Tywi like a line of verse
remembers wars, weathers, skulduggeries.

Below these broken walls ten centuries
pass like afternoons across the face
of this old battleground, where kite and crow

feed on history's carcase beside the flow
of mountain water. The river's psalm,
a luminous scrawl between the tidy farms

in monkish Latin or a poet's Welsh,
washes the fields at every wounded dawn
and bloody sunset, blesses broken bones

turned up by the plough and buried again
to lie a thousand springs under rising corn.

CHAWTON

In her room in the quiet house
her small table is a saucer
where her quick pen dips, her mind
in conversation with the world.

In the garden, flowers open their throats
to the rummage of bees, till dusk darkens
the page, and a last rush of starlings
scrawls its closing sentence on the sky.

In a hundred years, a hundred more,
a girl reading at a table laps the words
of every elegant line, each turned
page an opening door.

Reader, desire is the dark avenue
to Pemberley. You hardly breathe,
imagining the dance, a light hand laid
between your shoulder blades.

MAGNETISM

after Sonnet 116

Pull between earth and moon, or chemistry,
carries the swallow home from Africa
to perch again on his remembered tree,
the weeping birch by the pond. A star

will guide his mate home in a week, perhaps,
to the old nest in the barn, remade, mould
of spittle and pond-sludge snug in its cusp
as the new year in the mud-cup of the old.

Loss broke the swan on the river when winter
stole his mate while he wasn't looking. Believing,
he waited, rebuilt the nest, all summer
holding their stretch of river, raging, grieving.

So would I wait for you, were we put apart.
Mind, magnetism, hunger of the heart.

IRONING

I iron your shirts, fold each one because
you are work-weary and the world weeps.
Salt-breath of Atlantic grief in the rain
is a fine damp on collar and sleeve;

and the risen wind that filled with your spirit
the laundered shirt on the line,
is not breath of a broken father or child,
not the cry of a city for its dead.

I iron this sleeve, this cuff, because here
you will rest the pearl-bone of your wrist,
like a sea-smoothed stone for my soothing thumb,
here where your fingers fold on a flower,

a pen, a spade, gear stick of tractor or car,
or my shoulder, pressing me home.

Small sound like a water drop, a word sings
on my screen from god knows where:
one note from a scream of swallows;
the snap of a harp string on a warm evening,

and it's you, Yasmin, teacher from your English class
in Mianwali, Pakistan. Your girls' questions,
their hearts' hurt for the wounded one in the poem,
flown across the classroom of the world;

or you, Emmanuel, in your broken, African boy-talk,
text-speaking to me from your school in Accra, Ghana.
'Help me!' you say, you in your class of too many,
your hand raised to your teacher's praising surprise.

Our words, migrating the sky's blue road,
are swallows with African dust on their wings
the lightnings of Asia turning in blades of sunlight,
the taste of salt, this warm Atlantic morning.

WHITE LILIES

after a painting by Siani Rhys James

The lilies yawn like leopards
caged all day in the hot house.
Back late, we open the door
and an animal breath flows out,
filling the night-garden, bittersweet
with azalea and cat-breath of flowers.

Inside, paw-prints of pollens
the colour of blood, soft
blood-beads to stain the fingers,
a petal curled like a cat
on the scratched piano,
scent escaped like a gas.

I inhale it, dizzy, losing myself
in thickets of frond, fern, leaf,
stems and stamens of roses,
wallpaper flowers climbing the walls
of the yellow room, red room, blue room,
in a stink of nectar and damp.

They grow over the windows, the doors,
till I'm spellbound in the story
of a girl-woman tamed and trapped
in a tower in a wood in a thicket
of flowers, where something
is breathing, is purring, is prowling.

Remembering wind in the white oaks
I plant my chair in a wilderness, settle it neat
as a lark's nest in a cleft crushed in the grass
under buzzard and crow, the wind-blown flocks
of curlew, clouds, ideas, words.

Remembering cherries shaking foam from their hair.
I launch my chair on a wave for the spray on my page,
the taste of salt, the snap of a sail,
words homing in paragraphs over the sea,
a silver leap from the depths.

Remembering songs of chainsaw, chisel, plane,
I float my chair on a floor smooth as a lake,
its mind on reflections. I consider carpenters, makers,
hands silking the wood. A stipple of thought
surfaces like a trout, a tug on the line.

THE CENTURIES' POETRY:
HOPKINS TO ELIOT

Volume 5, 1954 – two shillings and sixpence

Dear Phyllis, what are you doing here, astray
on the shelves of Tŷ Newydd's library,
a hundred miles and seventy years away
from where you recited the world's poetry
in your rented rooms, in Carmarthen?

In your familiar hand your name, just here
in your usual blue *Quink*, or biro,
on postcards, letters, my Complete Shakespeare.
On my seventh birthday, before I knew the words,
your King James Bible sang wild songs –
'firmament', 'the deep', 'void', 'in the beginning',
lifting off silence like a rush of wings.

And here's dear Hopkins, 'sweet, sour, adazzle, dim',
And it was with you, aunt Phyllis, I first found him.

IN A CARDIFF ARCADE, 1952

One of those little shops too small
for the worlds they hold, where words
that sing you to sleep,
stories that stalk your dreams,
open like golden windows in a wall.

One small room leads to another,
the first bright-windowed on the street,
alluring, luminous. The other is dusk,
walled with pressed pages, old books
with leathery breath and freckled leaves.

What stays is not the book alone
but where you took it down,
how it felt in your hands,
how she wrapped it in brown paper,
how you carried it home,

how it holds wild seas
that knock the earth apart,
how words burn, freeze,
to break and heal your heart.

THE SCRIBE

Magna Carta

I choose my fifty plumes, each quill
a flight feather from the wing of a swan;
take pen, knife to shave it sharp as the steel
my father hones to cut the sod on the hill,
his furrow-long strip, his little acreage
worked with beam and blade under the sun,
a scrap of land laid open like my page,
scoured, stretched sheepskin ready for my pen.

I labour with my brother scribes till dusk,
sharpen the stylus to a beak and dip
in oak-gall crushed with soot, one sip
of ink at a time, bow to the task.
My heart beats to the Latin monotone
as I work my line to the end and turn
till my fingers cramp and my eyes burn.
Scribe, ploughman, each works his furrow alone.

Out in the garden and the singing woods,
the canticle of blackbird, psalm of thrush,
the season's holy offices from lauds
to vespers, an earthy bloodrush
of fertility to ease heart and hand.
When, in a hundred years, seven hundred more,
as summer spreads its long light on the land,
will this, my burden of scribed words, still stand?

In the twilit dome of the egg, the embryo's listening,
learning the refrain its parent sings.

A baby imagines a word's shape
before trying to speak, watches it on the lip

of whoever leans over the cot, hears it maze down the silk
of the ear, feels it settle in the tree of the brain,

tastes it in salts of skin, drinks it in milk,
spittle and tears, cries it in darkness and dream,

before tongue taps *d, t,* and lips unfold
from *la* to vowel, turning word to world.

Gwyneth Myfanwy, dying at ninety-three,
calls 'Mam! Oh! Mam!' from the landscape of her dream,

her sunlit story of ten decades past
retelling itself, her first word, her last.

VI

ELEGIES

September, he dips his beak in the lawn,
descendent of a mother bird long gone
to feathers on the wind, white bones.

He who sang through the summer of his life
from the summit of the ash, runs in the grass,
head cocked, tossing leaf-mould and mulch,

now stabs in silence, sounding the dark house of the worm
ghosting the song of love and possession,
holding ground, and winter coming.

*

They bore him hurt away
to be healed by miraculous fingers,
and lost like a great fish,
a slippery gleam of silver in the current
of a hospital corridor.

*

This is the dying season.
Birds hold their tongues.
Words wither in a yellow blaze
before they spin and fall,

blown by the wind
to shroud the wordless dead.
This is the sound
of no Seamus, Desmond, Dannie, Nigel.

Like a bird picking over
the September lawn,
I gather their leaves.
This is what silence is.

THE BROWN HARE

for R. S. Thomas

Never more than a shadow,
a silvering wind crossing a field,
two ears alert in a gap
then gone – its empty form

warm, like a room
someone just left,
its heart leaping the earth,
the silent immensities.

Once, on a cliff walk, we saw it,
a clod of clay in a saucer of grass
and the spaniel quivering
with scent of hare, with faith in hare,

quiet as dusk on the sea, its eye
a planet, the great muscle of its heart
gathering blood for the sprint,
a flight of sinew and gold, hot,

as if we could touch it, as if we could prove it,
as if you must place your hand
in the empty form to believe it,
as if the myth could be caged.

BARLEY

i.m. Dannie Abse

September, and all the way home in the train
I watch the gold unfolding fields of corn
the colour of Morfudd's hair, the land lit

with whisky ambers, ripeness bruised
by traces of a duller metal
where the wind ran, or a hare, or lovers have lain.

At the passing train, grief lifts from the land
on the wings of crows, and shadowless under the sun
the field where Dafydd marries his girl again.

As long as language lives and the wind's hand
fingers the harp strings of a golden field,
someone half dreaming in a train will listen

for remembered music of a line of verse,
and hear the barley whispering your words.

EISTEDDFOD OF THE BLACK CHAIR

for Hedd Wyn (1887–1917)

Robert Graves met him once,
in the hills above Harlech,
the shepherd poet,
the *awdl* and the *englyn* in his blood
like the *cynefin* of the mountain
in the breeding of his flock.

In a letter from France, he writes
of poplars whispering, the sun going down
among the foliage like an angel of fire.
and flowers half hidden in leaves
growing in a spent shell.
'Beauty is stronger than war.'

Yet he heard sorrow in the wind, foretold
blood in the rain reddening the fields
under the shadow of crows,
till he fell to his knees at Passchendaele,
grasping two fistfuls of earth, a shell to the stomach
opening its scarlet blossom.

At the Eisteddfod they called his name three times,
his audience waiting to rise, thrilled,
to crown him, chair him,
to sing the hymn of peace,
not 'the festival in tears and the poet in his grave',
a black sheet placed across the empty chair.

LAST LETTER HOME

i.m. Wilfred Owen (1893–1918)

At the forester's house that watchful night,
writing his letter home by candlelight
in the fug of the cellar, snug, dug in
among his smoking, snoring, sleeping men,
his mind was clear, seeing a horizon
of good tomorrows, war's sorrow done.
His mother would read these words at home, guns
fall silent, his men go home to wives and children.

The letter's lit with generosity,
coursing with light like the bright surface
of the Sambre canal where he would die
warning the world of war, leaving his words
on the white page of his grave, his voice
in the poetry of pity, the pity of poetry.

MADIBA

Nor Achilles, washed in waters of Styx, immortal
but for his infant heel held in his mother's hand.
Nor Hercules, son of Zeus, maddened a spell
by jealous Hera. Nor great Odysseus,
fierce for Athenians in the Trojan war,
Nor Theseus who killed the Minotaur.

He was Madiba, who raged but never blamed,
who was prepared to die for this, a dream:
all people will be free under the sun.
For this they held him twenty-seven years,
hard labour, solitude, islanded by seas.
Twenty-seven years.

He came out smiling to the world's applause.
Remember those patient lines, his people standing
hours under the African sun for his gift,
a slip of paper, a cross, a name, a right.
They queued in joy. Not long to wait
after waiting all their lives.

His final gift, his death.
Widow and estranged wife embrace.
Nations locked in hostility shake hands.
He made the lion lie down with the lamb.
He brought white doves to a weeping nation,
though he was no Arthur.

DAUGHTER

i.m. April Jones (2007–2012)
for Paul & Coral Jones

A pearl, April, born of water,
borne now in the river's arms,
child of the mountain,
mermaid of the estuary,
everyone's daughter.

Let her not be lost to the mothering sea.
Let her be light on the wave.
Let her change us forever.
Let us see her sweet face whenever
we gaze on the river, the sea,
like the moon on water.

Let this pain that is sleepless
lighten to love, to kindness.
Let ours be the arms that caught her,
love's weight, her light, the lightness
of everyone's daughter.

Olwen alone on the *Fan*. Where she goes
she leaves her prints like dustings of last snow,
or fallen petals where her white feet go,
and mist on the river is her breath's wild rose.

September silence. The blackbird's on the lawn
who sang all summer from the summit of the ash,
knew only a few acres of belonging,
but held his ground, possessed it with a psalm,
the *Veni, Vidi, Vici* of his song.

He sang in Auschwitz, though he knew nothing
of the mother whose sheared hair he stole
to bind his nest of moss and mud and grasses,
or her starved child watching behind the wire
the murderous purpose of the trucks.

Innocent, he sang in Srebrenica
from the spires of cypress, cedar, palm,
above the grave of slaughtered boys and men,
beloved bodies cast in despair's deep pit
and buried, nameless, without hymn or balm.

A bird's pure voice heard in the killing fields
while Cambodia's millions died, bodies thrown
like detritus into the wounded earth.
Now swallows in the evening air rehearse
their journey south above Rwanda and Darfur,

along familiar sky-roads in the air.
Men, women, children loved and were beloved,
maybe heard birdsong, words' song,
before the silence, and the blood,
before their names were prayer.

In the dream I held him in my arms,
a salt-soaked broken child calling my name.
Warm, real, all day he lives in me,
pulled from the collapsing rubble of the sea,
its grey, repetitive emptiness
like mercy's unbearable silence.

Last night we saved a wren, beguiled
by our Christmas room, trapped, terrified,
in from the *cwtch* of the old swallow's nest,
as cities and civilisations fall to dust
before our eyes, and every murdered child,
the old, the living, take to the dying road

while the whole weeping world
would save them, if it could.

NEW MOON

Venus in the arc of the young moon
is a boat in the arms of a bay,
the sky clear to infinity
but for the trailing gossamer
of a transatlantic plane.

The old year and the old era dead,
pushed burning out to sea
bearing the bones of heroes, tyrants,
ideologues, thieves and deceivers
in a smoke of burning money.

The dream is over. Glaciers will melt.
Seas will rise to swallow golden islands.
Somewhere a volcano may whelm a city,
earth shake its skin like an old horse,
a hurricane topple a town to rubble.

Yet tonight, under the cold beauty
of the moon and Venus, something like hope begins,
as if times can turn, the world change course.
Maybe black-hearted boys in love with death
won't blow themselves and us to smithereens,

guns fall silent, the powerful cease
slaughtering the weak, the rich will not gorge
as the poor starve. Maybe good men
will again come to power, truth speak,
and words have meaning again.

NOTES

PATAGONIA *hwyl fawr*: goodbye

HAFOD Y LLAN National Trust farm on Snowdon

RIVER *hafod* (shepherd's summer cottage) *hendre* (shepherd's winter house)

A YEAR AT HAFOD Y LLAN *saf yna! tyrd yma! cer ti ôl! / gan bwyll, gan bwyll! i'r de, i'r de* (calls to the dogs: 'Stay there! Come here! Go back. Easy. To the right') *from bwlch and cwm, crib and carreg* (from gap and valley, ridge and rock) *cân o'r mynyddoedd, sŵn drwmio, yn yr awyr, ar y trac* (song of the mountains, sound of drumming in the air, on the track) *cynefin* (heft, knowledge) *sŵn traed defaid ar y llwybrau, / sŵn dŵr dwfn dan y mynydd, / sŵn y gwynt ym mhyllau'r llechi* (sound of sheep's feet on the tracks / sound of deep water in the mountain / sound of wind in the slate mines) *cân bûr o bŵer yn Afon Cwmllan, / yn alcemi o ddŵr a thrydan* (pure song of power in the river Cwmllan / in alchemy of water to electricity)

OLD RAM *hafod and hendre, 'scubor and beudy* (summer dwelling and winter dwelling, barn and cowshed)

CYNEFIN *hiraeth* (longing)

SEPTEMBER *cân o'r mynyddoedd, / sŵn drwmio, yn yr awyr, ar y trac* (song of the mountains, / sound of drumming in the air, on the track)

WILD LABURNUM *tresi aur* (golden chain)

STORWM AWST (August Storm)

CANTRE'R GWAELOD a legendary country under Cardigan Bay

SYCHARTH *penillion* (lines of a poem with music) *llys* (hall)

THE CENTURIES' POETRY *Tŷ Newydd*: Writers Centre, Gwynedd

BARLEY Dafydd: Dafydd ap Gwylim, medieval poet; Morfudd: Dafydd ap Gwylim's lover

EISTEDDFOD OF THE BLACK CHAIR *awdl and englyn*: Welsh poetic forms; *cynefin* (heft)

ACKNOWLEDGEMENTS

Thanks are due to John McGrath and the National Theatre of Wales for the commission that led to the sequences of poems *Hafod-y Llan* and *A Year at Hafod y Llan*, performed on Snowdon in 2014, and to The National Trust at Hafod-y-Llan, Snowdon, for their welcome and help.

Special thanks are also due to the Museum of Zoology, Cambridge, for their support during and since my residency in 2015.

I would also like to thank the following publications, anthologies, festivals and organisations which commissioned, prompted or first published some of these poems: *Literature Wales*; Tŷ Newydd; the BBC; *The Guardian*; *Ploughshares* (US); *The New Statesman*; the Wilfred Owen Society; *Poetry Remembers*, edited by Carol Ann Duffy; Hay Festival; Bristol Romantic Poets Festival; Dinefŵr Festival; Sheffield Festival 2014; *All My Important Nothings*, edited by Maura Dooley (smith|doorstop, 2015); Lincoln 800: Magna Carta; 'Shore to Shore'; American Oak; The Woodland Trust; the Royal National Institute of Blind People; the Holocaust Memorial Committee. Warm thanks to Jenny Swann, who created Candlestick Press.